Baby Book

by Sara Midda

Workman Publishing · New York

ISBN-13: 978-0-7611-1229-7
Workman books are available at
special discounts when purchased in bulk
for premiums and sales promotions as
well as for fund-raising or educational use.
Special editions or book excerpts can
also be created to specification.
For details, contact the Special Sales Director
at the address below.

Workman Publishing Company, Inc.
225 Varick Street
New York, NY 10014-4381
www.workman.com

Manufactured in China

10   9   8   7

Names

Amedeo
~~ricaReiko~~ Amy
Tadeo Shineko
auradah Milton
Berdo Ignac
Gina
Marti Jardin
Faustin
Myriam Bernar
Michoko Akiko
Kan
Nada Uta
Rafael Chaim
Harry Hideo
gustus Shoji
Witold Etienne Claus
JeanMel Inga
hyne Bill Julie Stamos
Nelson
Kazuo Vladimir
nton Boris Eva
Edouard
Giuseppe John
Olga
Vikki
tha Elena Juliss
Alice Hank
Rafael Tamsin
Anton Fujita
bastin Theodora Rie
avia Dudley Irene
udolph Paula Ben
Alex Luis David
Mose Abigail
se Joshua Georg
Carla Mia Natasha
Axel Claus Akiko
Jun Isidore
Leon Ari Ann L Jean
Octavia Sam
Leon John Jo
Linda
anc Olive Darius
Christina Raphael
heopile Joan
ntoinelle Juan Avi
Amnon Bethan Bertha
Clara Freya
Alberto Olive
Herb
Sally Elijah Barbara
mold Carmen Nick
or Benji Angelique
tisha Jack Wolfgang
Basil Eitan Zachary Fred
Beatrice Rani
ilde Renata Avi
Susan Shashi Klaus
Jacqui Tiffany
Helmran Vincent
Sybil Luc The Serge
ola Francesk Elspeth
Emile
Darius Uschi
Duncan Yael
orchest Etta
Patrick Daniel
Dominique Malte

Tomoko
Francesca
Hugo Aloysius
Ella Duncan Chloe
Isabelle
Seamus Eugene Vittorio
Waki Lenzo
Ingeborg Naoma Avi
Ramon Simone Man
Giovanni Oka
Bessie Marina Simona
Frederica
Umberto Luz
Amedeo Jane
Eryl Junji William
Luigi Andre Lina
Sofie Taco Marcel
Piera Micha Hans
Mike Titus Renato
Jacob Audrey Toru
Gary Gloria
Miyuki Kash Grace
Carlo Lawrence
Fernando Emma
Ambrose
Thornton Martin
Guy Marit Henry
Katherine Rosa Tom
Meno Char
Gill Emiko Gary Ken
Leo Franco Gabrielle
Rebecca Teru Saltiana
Gwen Illian Pip
Ronnie Amber
Misako Michael
Tim Tatsuko Kimie
Lotte Julian
Antonio
Patricia Ubaldo
Sofia Anita
Rosemary Johnnie
Ethel
Pedro Jenn
Kathy Tatsuko Annie
Regina Jack
Dino Adam Pierre
Heinz Jess
Grace Fumi
Anake Jesse
Sincad Toby
Yoshika Giuseppe
Jago Sidney
Michanan Edward
Maurice Mari
Eda
Mordecai Edwin
Evelyn Simone
Max Giuseppina
Placido Gra
Zeb

NickNamES

Ancestor
Inventor
Great Great Relative
Grandad
Historical F
FRiEND
Father Aunt
Grandmother Bo
Liked name
Explorer Research
Gardener Painter
Doctor Uncle
Friend Hero
Journal Politician
Mother Scientist
Nurse
Heroine Writer
Musician Actor
Partner Compu
Biolog Musician
Cousin Cook
Sports Person
Flower
Biblical figure
Imaginary Town
Country
Colleague place
Designer Parent
Operatic figure
Illustrator
Cricketer Teacher
Prof Fairy Artist
Archaeo Craftsman
President Month
er in law Jewel Priest
Stone Rel
Season Engine Cou
A person liked
Sister star Botanist
Brother Compos
country Ballerina
Tree Singer
Relative
Herb Baby
Architect Plant
Date Distant Cousin
Inventor School Fri

Birth

22 23 24 1 2
21 3
20 4
19 5
18 6
17 7
16 8
15 9
14 13 12 11 10

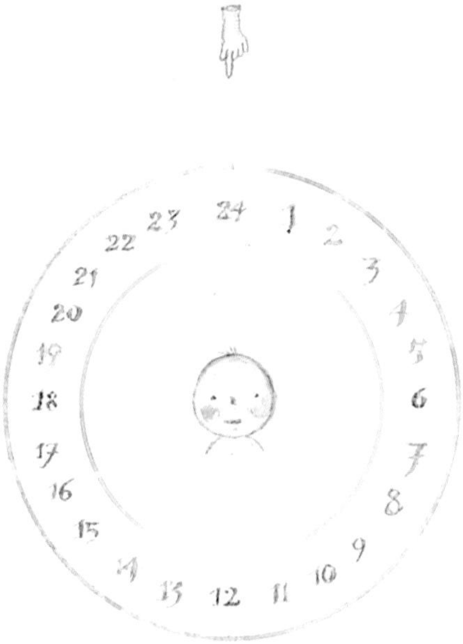

_____ — time

_____ date

_____ day

_____ month

_____ year

1
2
3
4
5
6
7
8
9
10
11
12
13
14
15
16
17
18
19
20
21
22
23
24
25
26
27
28
29
30
31

WEight

Height

at birth

one month

two months

three months

four months

five months

six months

seven months

eight months

nine months

ten months

eleven months

twelve months

eighteen months

two years

five years

eighty-five years

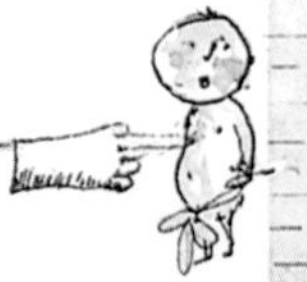

Hair

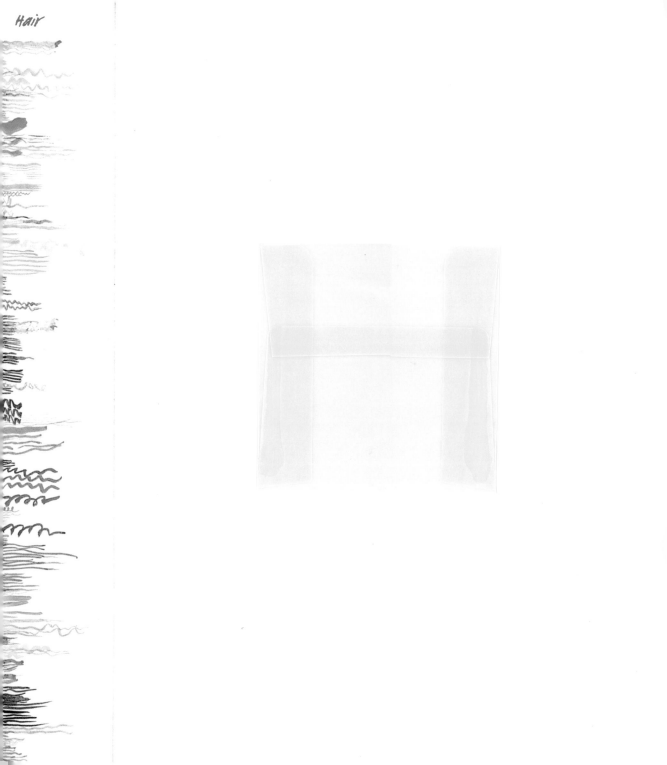

Skin/Eyes

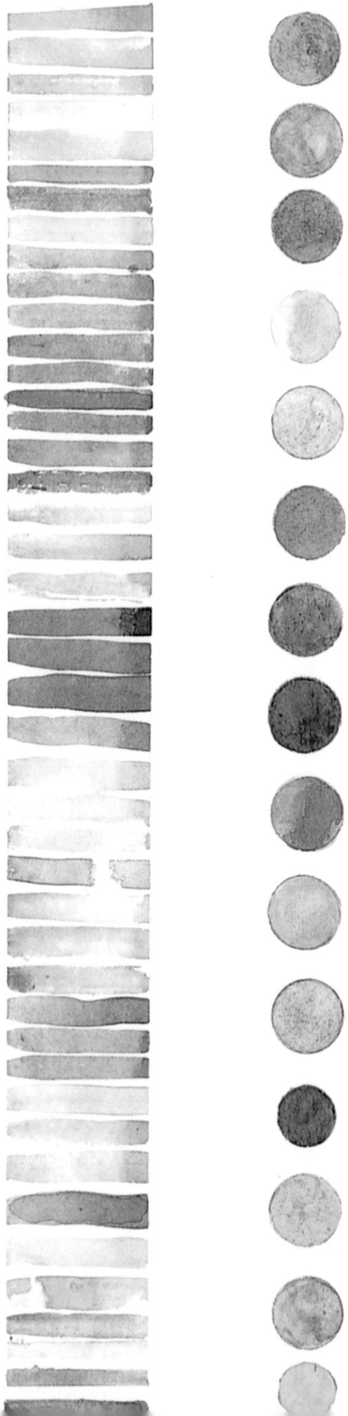

NEWSPAPER
Announcement

BIRTH

visitors

Photos

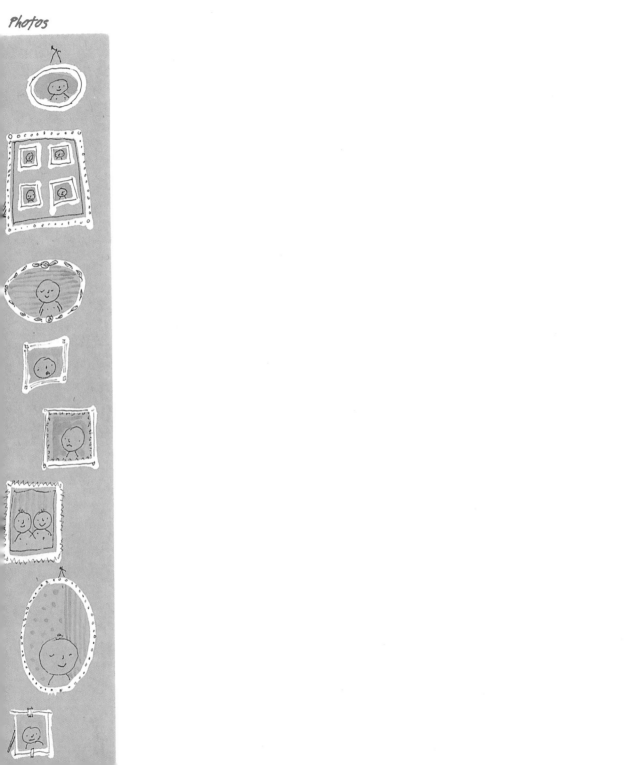

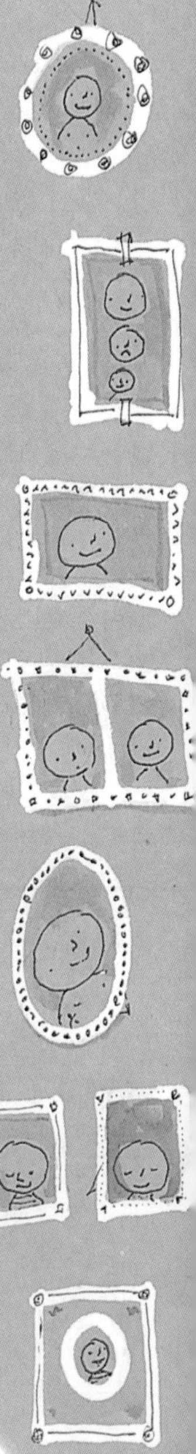

First Day

mother

Siblings

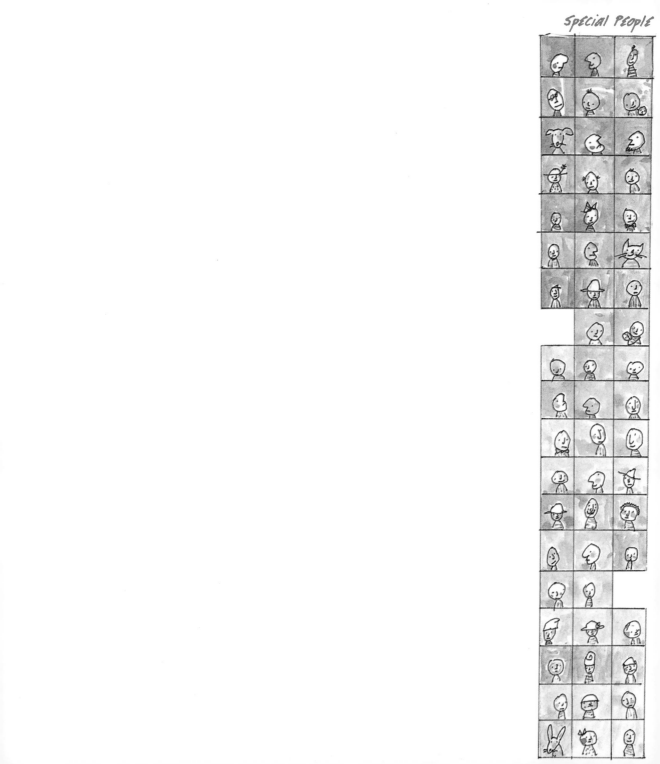

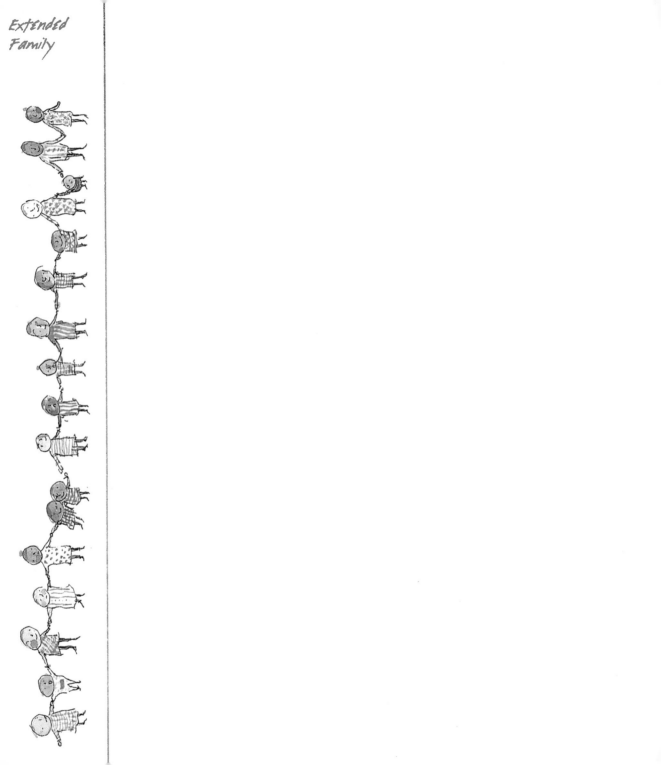

Extended
Family

Religious
Ceremonies

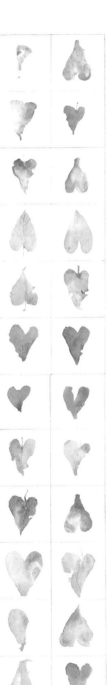

Sign of the...

SLEEping

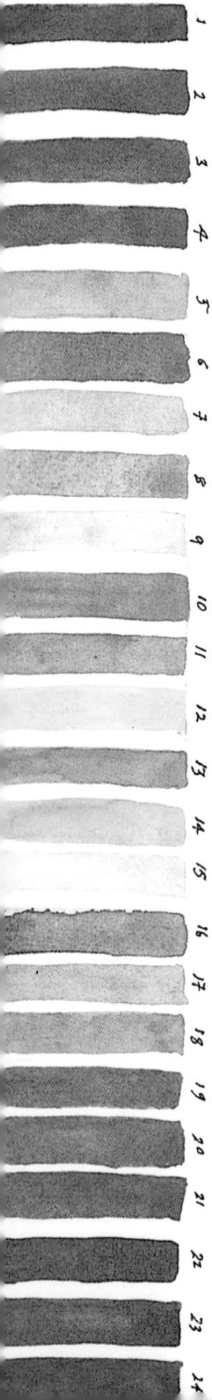

1
2
3
4
5
6
7
8
9
10
11
12
13
14
15
16
17
18
19
20
21
22
23
24

first night

second night

third night

fourth night

fifth night

sixth night

seventh night

First night slept through

Milk of Choice

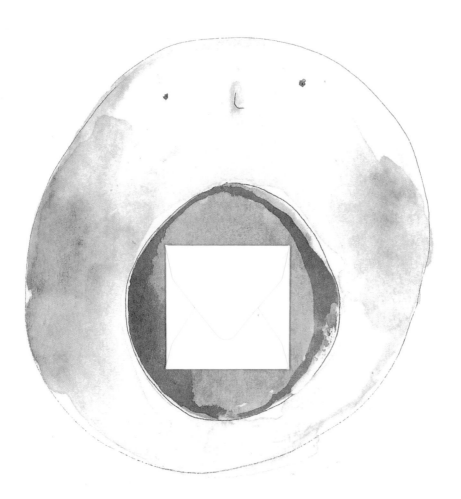

First seen · · · · · · · · · · · ·
Became wobbly · · · · · · · · · ·
Came out · · · · · · · · · · · ·

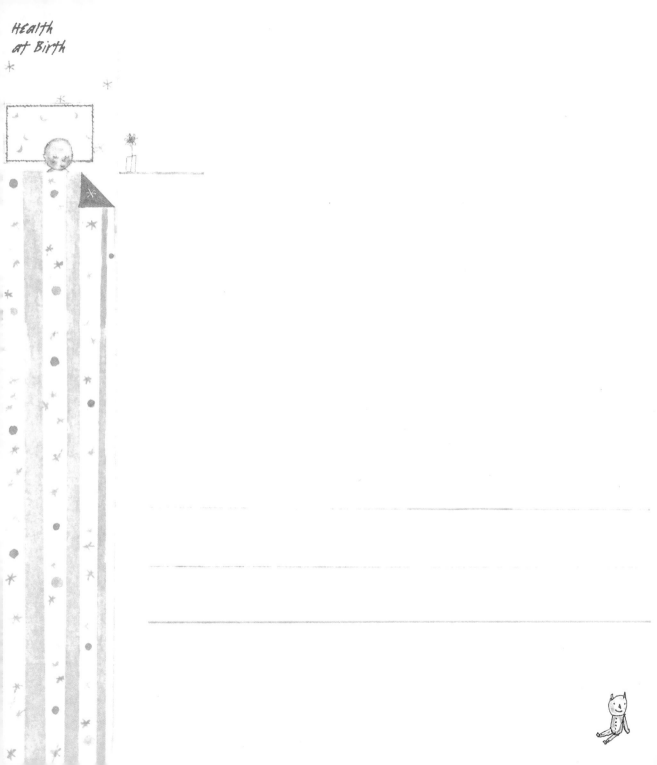

Health
at Birth

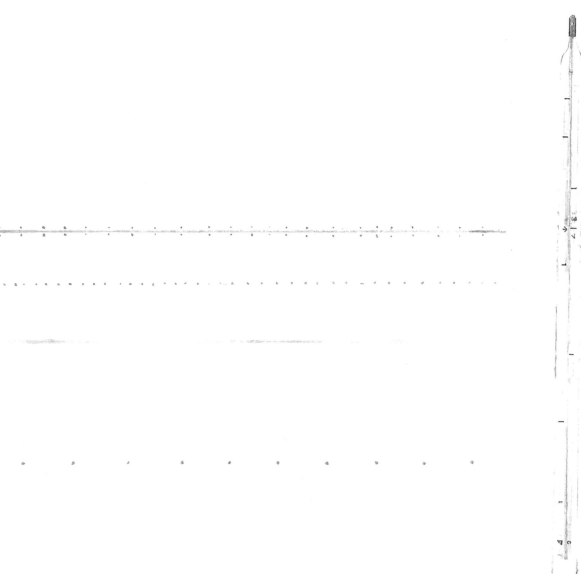

HOMES

Response to
weather

Things that
made me sad

Things that
made me happy

Fears

Personality

SEEing

Photos

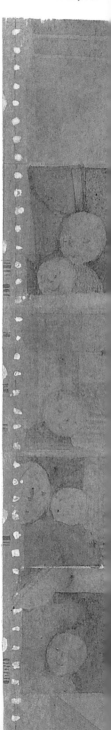

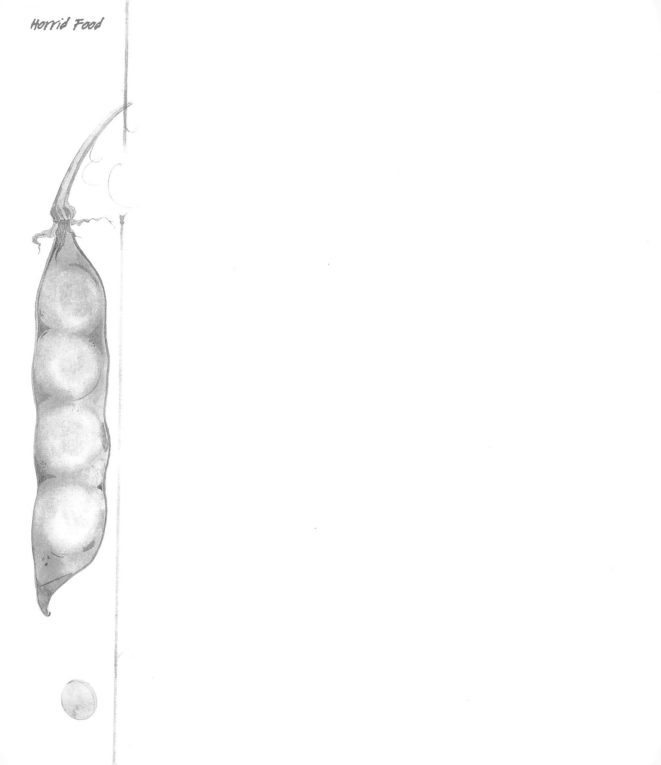

PETS

Lullabies

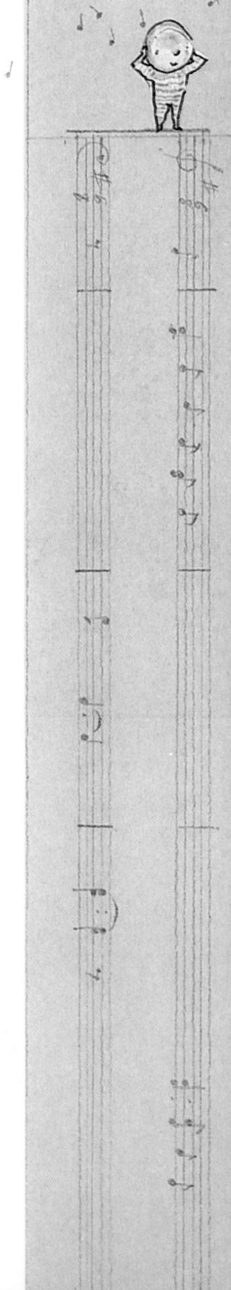

Private
Language

ABCDEFGH ijklm nopqrstuvwxyz

Clothes

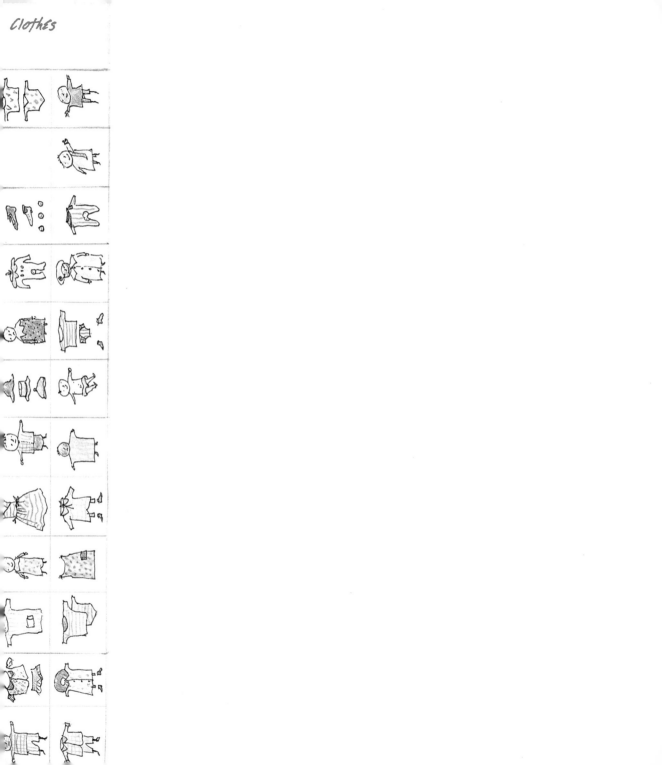

Toys

5
9
3

8

14   6

11

First Words

First Words

Frustrations

BEDTIME
Rituals

Early Art

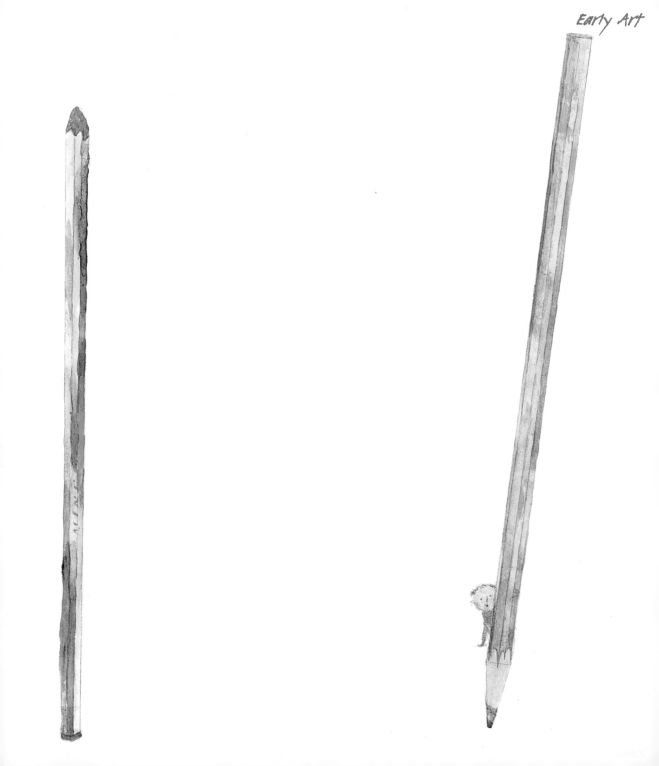

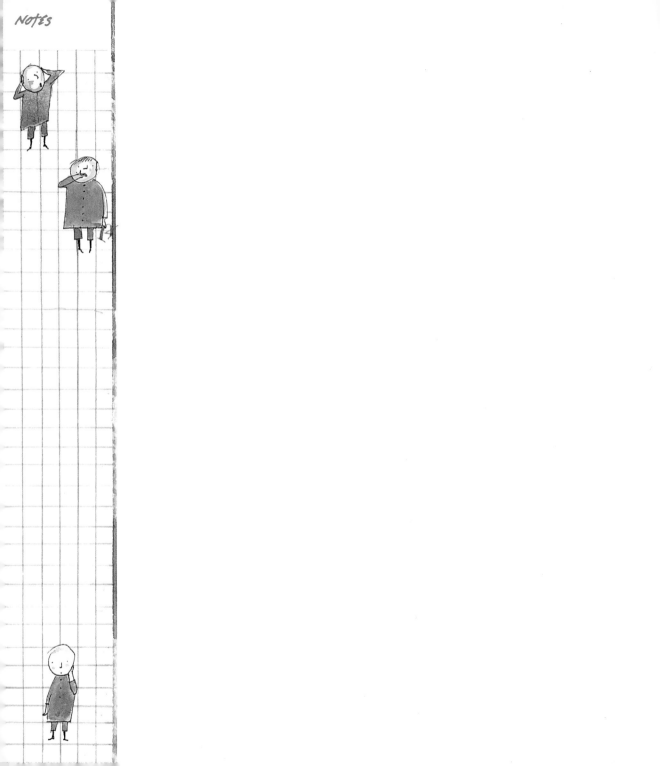

First Birthday

First Birthday

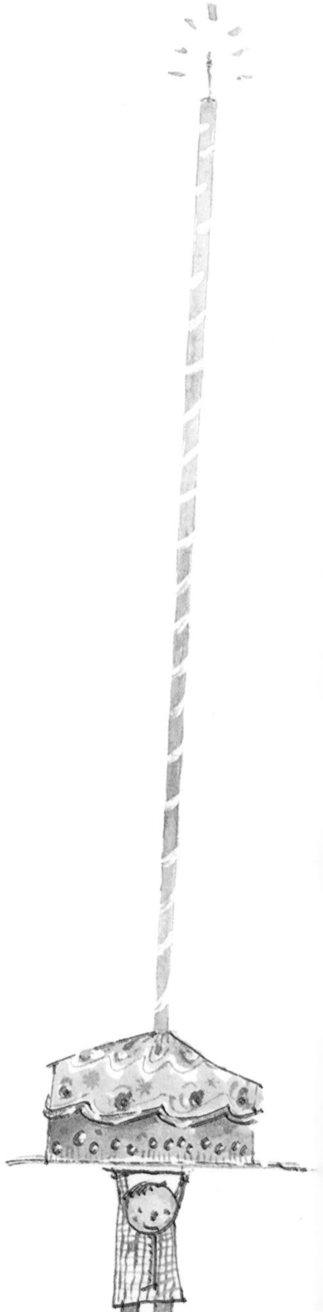

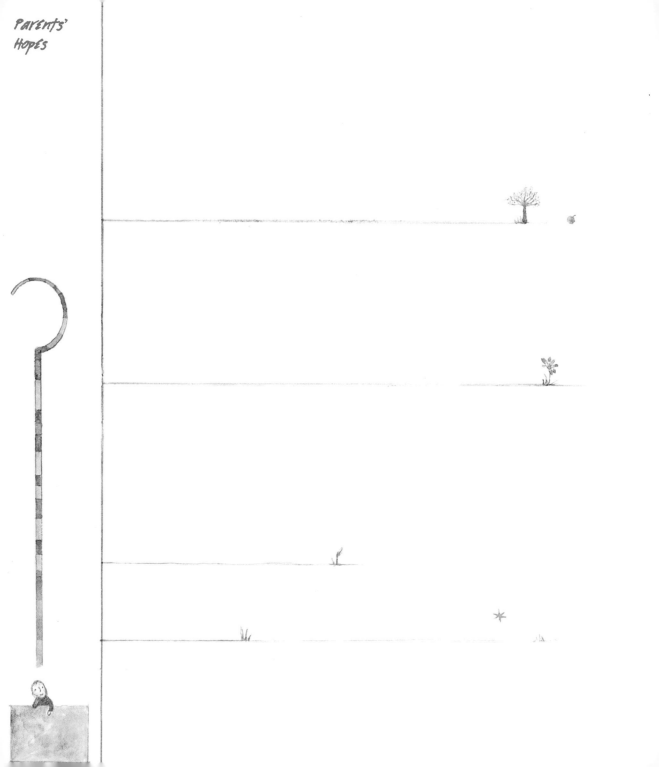

NOTES

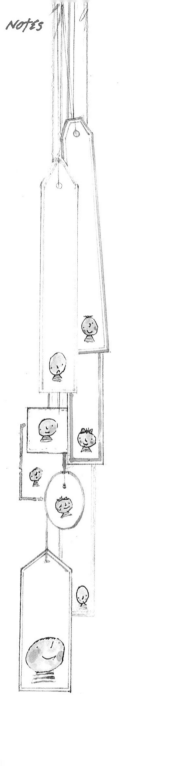

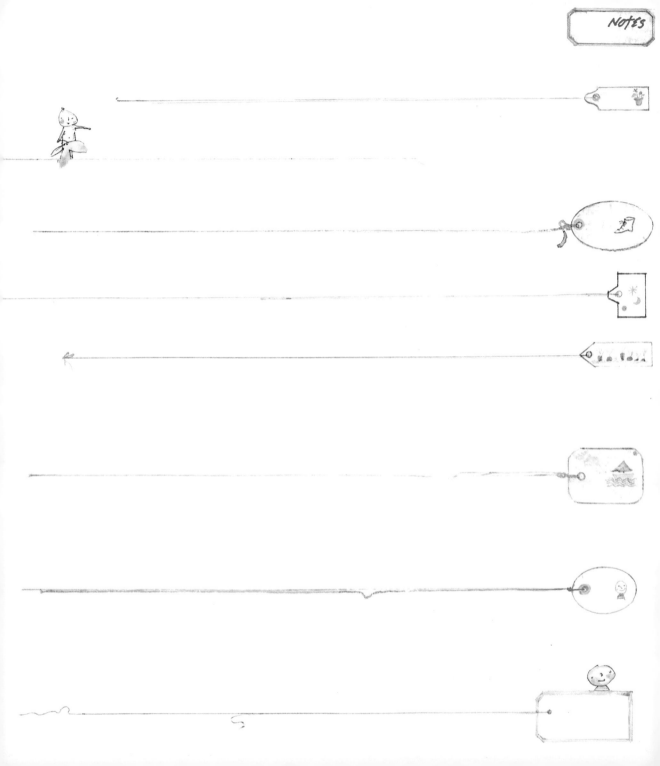

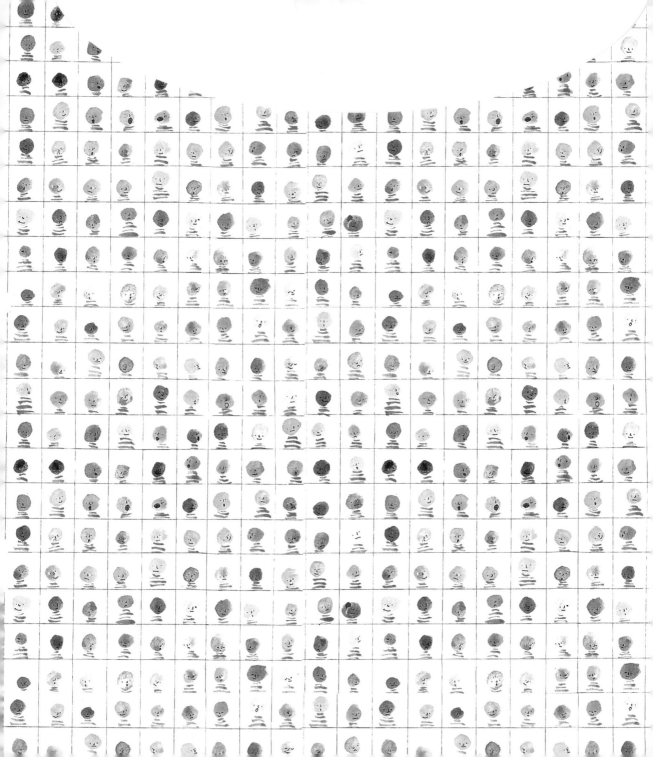